POWER
&
FRUIT
of the
HOLY
SPIRIT

POWER & FRUIT of the HOLY SPIRIT

An Eleven-Week Guide for Group Bible Study

Bruce Williams

Power and Fruit of the Holy Spirit
© 2005 by Discipleship Publications International

300 Fifth Avenue
Fifth Floor
Waltham, Massachusetts 02451

All rights reserved.

No part of this book may be duplicated, copied, translated,
reproduced or stored mechanically or electronically
without specific, written permission of Discipleship Publications
International.

All Scripture quotations, unless indicated, are taken from
the NEW INTERNATIONAL VERSION.
Copyright ©1973, 1978, 1984 by the International Bible Society.
Used by permission of Zondervan Publishing House.
All rights reserved.

The "NIV" and "New International Version" trademarks
are registered in the United States Patent Trademark Office
by the International Bible Society.
Use of either trademark requires the permission of
the International Bible Society.

Printed in the United States of America

Cover photo: Brand X Pictures

ISBN: 1-57782-202-1

Contents

INTRODUCTION:	From the Author	6
WEEK ONE:	Maximum Power	7
WEEK TWO:	God's Expectations	13
WEEK THREE:	The Fruit of the Spirit is LOVE	21
WEEK FOUR:	The Fruit of the Spirit is JOY	29
WEEK FIVE:	The Fruit of the Spirit is PEACE	35
WEEK SIX:	The Fruit of the Spirit is PATIENCE	41
WEEK SEVEN:	The Fruit of the Spirit is KINDNESS	47
WEEK EIGHT:	The Fruit of the Spirit is GOODNESS	53
WEEK NINE:	The Fruit of the Spirit is FAITHFULNESS	57
WEEK TEN:	The Fruit of the Spirit is GENTLENESS	61
WEEK ELEVEN:	The Fruit of the Spirit is SELF-CONTROL	65
EPILOGUE:	Walking in the Spirit	71

INTRODUCTION

FROM THE AUTHOR

This book contains a series of lessons on the amazing power that we have through the Holy Spirit and the fruit that is borne from the Spirit. As a people of God, we have not only been promised forgiveness of every sin we have ever committed (which is extraordinary), but we have also been given power to be transformed, which is even more phenomenal!

In this series of lessons, you will see that there are a prolific number of passages in God's word that detail God's tremendous promises and expectations. I pray that these studies will feed your soul and encourage your spirit. I also pray that they will increase your daily appetite and thirst for the word of God.

These studies are intended to be read prior to meeting with your small group. After reading through the study, I encourage you to take some time to reflect and meditate: "I meditate on your precepts and consider your ways" (Psalm 119:15). Reflection gives the Lord an opportunity to give us greater wisdom. "Reflect on what I am saying, for the Lord will give you insight into all this" (2 Timothy 2:7).

Please don't forget to claim and enjoy the fruit of the Spirit! There is no one who wants us to truly live joyful and fulfilling lives more than God and his Spirit. Let the light of his Spirit shine through your life and heart!

> And we, who with unveiled faces all reflect the Lord's glory, are being transformed into his likeness with ever-increasing glory, which comes from the Lord, who is the Spirit. (2 Corinthians 3:18)

Bruce Williams

WEEK ONE

MAXIMUM POWER

Simon Peter, a servant and apostle of Jesus Christ, To those who through the righteousness of our God and Savior Jesus Christ have received a faith as precious as ours: Grace and peace be yours in abundance through the knowledge of God and of Jesus our Lord. His divine power has given us everything we need for life and godliness through our knowledge of him who called us by his own glory and goodness. Through these he has given us his very great and precious promises, so that through them you may participate in the divine nature and escape the corruption in the world caused by evil desires.

2 Peter 1:1–4

1. To whom is the passage written?
   - To _____ who through the righteousness of our God and Savior Jesus Christ have received a _____ as precious as ours. (1:1)
   - In other words, all true Christians.

2. According to this verse, what kind of power do we, as disciples, have?
   - His _____ power. (1:3)

3. What are the limits of this power?
   - His divine power has given us _____ we need for _____ and _____. (1:3)
   - ...so that you may participate in the _____ _____ and escape the _____ of the world caused by _____ _____. (1:4)
   - So is there a limit to this power? _____

Take just a moment to reflect on how amazing that is. What an incredible gift the Lord has given us! He has not just given us some mediocre power in our lives. When we go out and buy batteries for our CD player, we don't ask the salesperson to show us batteries that have the least amount of power. We want the maximum power available.

Why? Because we don't want to run out! That is what the Lord has given us: *maximum power*. It's all the power we will ever need!

Here's something for you to think about: we never need to pray for more power! We will never need a recharge! "His divine power has [already] given us everything we need for life and godliness" (1:3). How can he give us any more? The only thing that may need to be "recharged" is our commitment to him or our surrender to him; we have not run out of power, but maybe focus, desire and a willingness to let the power be released.

Now let us go see where this incredible power comes from:

> You, however, are controlled not by the sinful nature but by the Spirit, if the Spirit of God lives in you. And if anyone does not have the Spirit of Christ, he does not belong to Christ. But if Christ is in you, your body is dead because of sin, yet your spirit is alive because of righteousness. And if the Spirit of him who raised Jesus from the dead is living in you, he who raised Christ from the dead will also give life to your mortal bodies through his Spirit, who lives in you.
>
> Therefore, brothers, we have an obligation—but it is not to the sinful nature, to live according to it. For if you live according to the sinful nature, you will die; but if by the Spirit you put to death the misdeeds of the body, you will live, because those who are led by the Spirit of God are sons of God. (Romans 8:9–14)

1. In Romans 8:9, there are actually three terms (or names) given for who lives inside of us. What are they?
   - The _____. (8:9)
   - The _____ _____ _____. (8:9)
   - The _____ _____ _____. (8:9)
2. When do we receive this Holy Spirit into our lives? (Acts 2:38)
   - After we _____ and are _____.

When we repent and are baptized, all of our sins are washed completely away, not by the water, but by putting us spiritually in contact with the death (blood) of Jesus Christ, and the resurrection of Jesus Christ, as we are immersed into that water (1 Peter 3:21).

But that is not all that happens at baptism. We are also given the power of the Holy Spirit! (Acts 2:38). That is why this entire event is described by Jesus as being "born again" (John 3:7) "of the water and the Spirit" (John 3:5).

This _____ birth is a requirement to get into the kingdom (John 3:3, 5, 7). God knew that forgiveness would not be enough for a new life. He needed to give us divine power in order for the old life and self to truly be put behind us and for the new life and self to emerge (Romans 6:4).

We have examined the kind of power that is available to all of us who have truly been united with Christ by repenting of our sins and being baptized into Christ. God has made this amazing power available to every single one of us. He has promised in his word that he has not left us powerless and on our own to overcome sin and make changes in our lives. We have to assume that he has put these promises of power in his word to encourage our souls and inspire our hearts. He obviously wants us to be aware and convinced of this fact: we have divine power!

Meditation and Discussion Questions

1. Do you believe you have divine power? If yes, why? If no, why not?

2. Consider the changes in your life that have come as a result of having divine power.
   • List the characteristics you now have due to this maximum power.

   • What weaknesses did you overcome as a result of the Holy Spirit?

3. What changes stand out to you that you still need to make (just name a few)?

4. Have you ever prayed for more power? After looking at these passages, what do you believe you should be praying for?

5. How much do you reflect upon and remind yourself of this power?

6. What will be different in your life this week as a result of this study?

7. How will your counseling and training of fellow Christians be affected by this study?

– *Additional Notes* –

WEEK TWO

GOD'S EXPECTATIONS

In our previous lesson, we focused on the kind of power that is available to all of us who have truly been united with Christ by repenting of our sins and being baptized into him (Acts 2:38). He has promised in his word that he has not left us powerless and on our own. With all this divine power, are there any expectations?

> For this very reason, make every effort to add to your faith goodness; and to goodness, knowledge; and to knowledge, self-control; and to self-control, perseverance; and to perseverance, godliness; and to godliness, brotherly kindness; and to brotherly kindness, love. For if you possess these qualities in increasing measure, they will keep you from being ineffective and unproductive in your knowledge of our Lord Jesus Christ. But if anyone does not have them, he is nearsighted and blind, and has forgotten that he has been cleansed from his past sins.
>
> Therefore, my brothers, be all the more eager to make your calling and election sure. For if you do these things, you will never fall, and you will receive a rich welcome into the eternal kingdom of our Lord and Savior Jesus Christ. (2 Peter 1:5–11)

How do we make these changes?

We "make _____ _____" to grow (1:5).

Many times we hear religious people (and some preachers) say that our growth and change is all up to God—man has nothing to do with it. We are told that change is not about man's effort, but only God's power. Even though that sounds humble and spiritual, this passage does not support that theology. It is not all about God or all about us; it really involves both God and us. He provides the power ("For this very reason"), but we are to "make every _____ to _____." (1:5)

The word translated "make every effort" is the same root word in the Greek found in 2 Timothy 2:15 that is translated "do your best." Now that God has provided all this amazing power, he expects transformation; this is a great responsibility, but also one of the greatest blessings we have to share with others. Being born again is about being forgiven *and* receiving divine power so that we can actually live a new and different life.

I appreciate the increased emphasis on the grace of God in much of the preaching and teaching in the last couple of years. Some were not grounded in the love and patience of God and therefore lived in a constant state of guilt and insecurity. We need to make sure that the message of God's grace comes through loudly and clearly. I have observed some, however, who emphasize grace to the exclusion of personal responsibility and effort. You will never see that imbalance in the Scriptures unless you take certain verses out of context. Some have mistakenly thought (and taught) that if we just focus on the grace, change and fruit will automatically appear; that is not the message that God inspired Peter to write here in 2 Peter 1. He apparently saw the need to emphasize the need for every Christian to make every effort. There is an effort on our part that is emphasized and required.

As you look over the past year, how much effort have you put into growing spiritually? Can you honestly describe it as "making every effort"? How does it compare to other years as a Christian? Does God really expect this every year—year in and year out? The truth is that we cannot spiritually tread water for very long; the current of evil is too strong. I have witnessed strong Christians who were pulled back into the world and experienced spiritual disaster because they just felt like they deserved to take a break from "making all this effort."

Please note the expected progression of our growth: we are to "possess these qualities (faith, goodness, godliness…) in _____ measure" (1:8). Living the Christian life is not about being sinless, but

GOD'S EXPECTATIONS

about growing and making progress. We should be encouraged by the fact that no matter how long we are in the Lord, we can still change! Often when people get older, we find they get "set in their ways"; in other words, they are not open to learning much of anything new and not open to changing. One of the saddest pictures is of a family where the parents and grandparents are alienated from their children's families because of the unwillingness of the older to grow and make changes. Conversely, one of the most inspiring things about the Christian life is seeing growth and change in people from one year to the next, regardless of their age. Relationships cannot grow if individuals do not grow. Growth is promised when we make every effort.

God also promises that possessing these qualities in increasing measure (growing) keeps us from being _____ and _____ (1:8). We want our lives to count. We want to make a difference. These were some of my most compelling motivations to become a Christian and share my faith. I really wanted to make a difference with my life. I wanted it to have impact. As I studied the Scriptures more, I realized that God wanted the same thing for my life! He wants all of our lives to make an impact, to be effective and productive!

We set our minds on pleasing God.

> Those who live according to the sinful nature have their _____ set on what that nature desires; but those who live in accordance with the Spirit have their _____ set on what the Spirit desires. The _____ of sinful man is death, but the _____ controlled by the Spirit is life and peace; the sinful _____ is hostile to God. It does not submit to God's law, nor can it do so. Those controlled by the sinful nature cannot please God.
>
> You, however, are controlled not by the sinful nature but by the Spirit, if the Spirit of God lives in you. And if anyone does not have the Spirit of Christ, he does not belong to Christ. But if Christ is in you, your body is dead because of sin, yet your spirit is alive because of righteousness. And if the Spirit of him who

> raised Jesus from the dead is living in you, he who raised Christ from the dead will also give life to your mortal bodies through his Spirit, who lives in you.
>
> Therefore, brothers, we have an obligation—but it is not to the sinful nature, to live according to it. For if you live according to the sinful nature, you will die; but if by the Spirit you put to death the misdeeds of the body, you will live, because those who are led by the Spirit of God are sons of God. (Romans 8:5–14)

This great passage assures us that we have the same power that _____ Jesus from the dead (8:11). Because of that, what is our obligation? (8:12–13). It is to put to _____ the _____ of the body, and by doing so, you will _____! Living a life that pleases God begins with where we set our _____ (8:5). The sinful mind is _____ to God (8:7). In contrast, "the mind controlled by the Spirit is _____ and _____" (8:6). When we focus on pleasing God, our mind can be influenced by the Spirit (same as being spiritually minded).

I would encourage us to examine how much we think about pleasing God. We are all inspired by the apostle Paul's dramatic changes and his continual spiritual growth. What was it that consumed him?

> So we make it our goal to _____ him. (2 Corinthians 5:9)

> And we pray this in order that you may live a life worthy of the Lord and may _____ him in every way. (Colossians 1:10)

Most people have only one person they are really consumed with pleasing: themselves. It is not uncommon to hear, "Does this make me happy?" or "Is this what I want to do?" or "I have to do what feels right to me." Does this sound like someone who really is focused on pleasing the Lord? Unfortunately, pleasing God is not the basis from which most decisions are made. In fact, it is the furthest thing from most people's minds.

When we become disciples, pleasing the Lord needs to become the most important thing in our minds: "Finally, brothers, we instructed you how to live in order to *please* God, as in fact you are living" (1 Thessalonians 4:1, emphasis added). Pleasing God needs to be where our mind is set! When you set your mind on pleasing him, you will be amazed at how much more power and motivation comes into your life to do things you never thought possible.

Meditation and Discussion Questions

1. What stands out to you about God's expectations?

2. How does the world tempt us to doubt we can grow or change?

3. Think about the brothers or sisters who have been an example of tremendous growth.
   • Who are they and how was their growth demonstrated?

4. Think about this past year…
   • In what areas did you make significant spiritual changes and growth?

- What did you do and not do that enabled the Holy Spirit to help you to grow?

- How would you describe the effort that you made to grow?

5. Name two areas you need to begin to make every effort to grow in.

- What will you do differently in order to make every effort?

6. How much has pleasing God been the basis for your decisions this past year?

- Do you feel compelled to evaluate things with a different mindset in the future? Why or why not?

– Additional Notes –

WEEK THREE

The Fruit of the Spirit is LOVE

> But the fruit of the Spirit is *love*, joy, peace, patience, kindness, goodness, faithfulness, gentleness and self-control.
> Galatians 5:22–23, emphasis added

The first fruit of the Spirit is love; the Greek word is *agape*. In the New Testament, two of the Greek words that are translated as "love" are *agape* and *phileo*. *Phileo* is a word that is rooted in friendship and feelings of camaraderie and warmth. It is used 25 times in the New Testament. It is interesting that *phileo* is the Greek word that Judas used that is translated "kissed": "Going at once to Jesus, Judas said, 'Greetings, Rabbi!' and kissed him" (Matthew 26:49). The noun form of the word is *philos* and is translated "friend(s)" in each of the 29 passages in the NIV translation. It is used by Jesus and others to express his warmth and partnership with his disciples ("You are my friends (*philos*)..." John 15:14; "I have called you friends (*philos*)..." John 15:15.)

The more frequently used Greek word that is translated "love" is *agape*; it is used as a noun 117 times and 140 times in the verb form (*agapao*) in the New Testament. This is the first quality that is mentioned as a fruit of the Spirit.

> But I tell you: Love (*agapao*) your enemies and pray for those who persecute you, that you may be sons of your Father in heaven. He causes his sun to rise on the evil and the good, and sends rain on the righteous and the unrighteous. If you love those who love you, what reward will you get? Are not even the tax collectors doing that? And if you greet only your brothers, what are you doing more than others? Do not even pagans do that? Be perfect, therefore, as your heavenly Father is perfect. (Matthew 5:44–48)

Agape is a love that is not conditioned on how much the person deserves the love or how they respond to that love; it is truly unconditional. Unconditional love is without a doubt the most difficult kind of love to give to one another; it is not what comes naturally for any of us. Our natural inclination is to love those who love us in return and to despise (or at least be indifferent toward) those who do not. But we are not called to do just what comes naturally. ("If you love those who love you, what reward will you get? Are not even the tax collectors doing that?" Matthew 5:46.)

We are expected by God to go beyond our momentary feelings when it comes to relationships. Feelings are so unstable and unpredictable. When you really think about it, sometimes feelings can even be affected by what you had to eat the night before! I'm being a little facetious, but I think you get the picture. Feeling-based love in relationships is not what a marriage, a family or a lasting friendship can be built upon. Feelings are like the weather—wait long enough and they will change. Commitment and decision with heart must define our love for one another; those are the elements necessary to unconditional love. If our love is in any way conditional, then our relationships will be adversely affected. What sets us apart from the world is not our *phileo* (reciprocal love), but our *agapao*; this distinguishes us as "children of God." ("Love your enemies… _____ you may be sons of your Father in heaven" Matthew 5:44–45.)

At this point, you may be thinking, "That sounds fake, pretending to love someone you have no feelings for." This is where we can get manipulated by the demons in our thinking; the truth is we are only being fake if we claim to have feelings that are not there. Can you have love without the feeling of love? If our answer were based on Hollywood's definition of love, then our answer would have to be "no"; but God says, "Of course you can." Every time a parent gets up from a deep sleep in the middle of the night to attend to a crying baby, he or she is loving that child. Are there warm, fuzzy feelings for that baby at that moment in the middle of the night? Not usually. But is it an act of love? Yes, because it is not feeling-based, but commitment/decision-based love. You decide to love that child in spite of your feelings (your desire to stay in bed).

We can give love as an act of will, whether the feelings are there or not. Feelings do not define *agape*. That is why Jesus could command, "Love your enemies…" and truly expect us to obey it. You cannot force yourself to have feelings of love for your enemies, but you can choose to do loving things towards them based on a heartfelt decision, not on a feeling.

There are several places where we will be challenged to love like this almost every day. If you are married, then you have already had daily opportunities to deny your feelings (self) and show unconditional love for your spouse. This is especially true after several years of marriage and the euphoria of being newlyweds has passed; the inspiration to give, serve, compromise and forgive is not immediate and automatic, and you may wonder what happened to your prince or princess.

I'm sure that I have given Robyn plenty of opportunities to show *agape*. I'm not always as kind and considerate as I should be when I ask her to do something for me. I know I have taken for granted her daily acts of service that so easily go unnoticed except when they are not done. I don't encourage enough, praise enough, compliment enough, notice enough and express enough. But because Robyn is a disciple of Jesus Christ, her love for me is not conditional on how perfectly I praise, thank or notice. It is certainly encouraging to her when I do thank and notice (and I'm getting better), but her *agape* is not conditional on me and my reaction (thank God). As the ones who give love, our focus must be on how God expects us to give and to love, not on how others notice, appreciate or reciprocate. Parents are certainly expected to give *agape* from the minute their child is born. If a parent's love ever moves from unconditional to conditional, he or she will fail as a parent.

> For God so _____ the world that he _____ his one and only Son, that whoever believes in him shall not perish but have eternal life. (John 3:16)

People outside of Christ will give us the most opportunities to show *agape* because they often do not reciprocate. This is exactly the kind of love that was demonstrated at Calvary and turned the world on its heels: "For God so loved (*agapao*) the world…" In our outreach to the lost, our love will not usually be motivated or inspired through initial reactions. Our focus and motivation will have to be rooted in how much God has unconditionally loved us and how much others have unconditionally loved us to bring us to know God. This fruit of the Spirit will absolutely melt hardened hearts.

"For God so loved the world that he _____ .…" We do not truly show *agape* until we invest in people. Those outside of Christ desperately need to become more to us than just a passing thought, more than people we initiate with once or twice. Most of us who were converted required multiple phone calls, invitations, meals and follow-ups before having much interest in making a commitment to Christ. When you think about it, the world was neither significantly nor permanently turned to Christ by his miracles, as great and as powerful as they were. Even his disciples did not become loyal until after Jesus' ultimate display of *agape* at the cross and resurrection; as the ancient hymn expresses, "At the cross, at the cross, where I first saw the light…"

> A new command I give you: Love (*agapao*) one another. As I have loved you, so you must love one another. By this all men will know that you are my disciples, if you love one another. (John 13:34–35)

In order to be Jesus' disciples, we are commanded to love as he loved. People truly do not care how much we know, until they know how much we care. When we look at Jesus' life, death and resurrection, we see a man who never stopped extending, initiating and building relationships with the lost world; that is the way *agape* affects us; it compels us to keep on initiating and building so that others can see and know God's amazing grace.

Meditation and Discussion Questions

1. How much has God unconditionally loved you? How many times has he forgiven you for the same sins?

2. What stands out to you about the way Jesus practiced *agape*?

    • In what ways will you make a commitment to imitate him in expressing *agape*?

3. Think of the times when you have been unconditionally loved by other Christians.
    • Perhaps it was when you first came to Christ, or maybe later when you made it difficult to be loved.

- What demonstrated to you that their love was *agape*?

4. Think of the times when you have unconditionally loved others. Who were they and how did you demonstrate that love?

5. Think about the past month...
    - When you were victorious in demonstrating *agape*, what did you do and not do that enabled the Holy Spirit to give you unconditional love?

    - When you were not victorious in demonstrating *agape*, what did you do and not do that prevented the Holy Spirit from giving you unconditional love?

6. Identify the ones that still need to see more unconditional love from you. They may be family, friends, non-Christians or fellow Christians.

- What will you do to demonstrate more *agape*?

7. Is there anyone that you need to apologize to for not unconditionally loving them?

– *Additional Notes* –

WEEK FOUR

The Fruit of the Spirit is JOY

> But the fruit of the Spirit is love, *joy*, peace, patience, kindness, goodness, faithfulness, gentleness and self-control.
> Galatians 5:22–23, emphasis added

The second fruit of the Spirit is joy. The word in the Greek is *chara* (khar-ah). It means "exceeding joy—overflowing joy." It is the same word that Jesus used in telling us the reward of those who multiplied their talents. ("...come and share your Master's happiness (*chara*) Matthew 25:21, 23). The verb form of this root word is usually translated "rejoice."

The apostle Paul uses either the verb or the noun of this root word 14 times in the book of Philippians alone. Paul has grabbed ahold of this fruit. He made a decision that it would define him as much as any other.

As you read about Paul and his life, you get the impression that this man approaches life with intensity! He never appears to have done anything half-hearted. He goes from persecuting Christians to laying down his life for them. Even though he redirected his intense personality for God, something else was also radically different: he really begins to enjoy his life! And why shouldn't he? His purpose is no longer to badger, persecute and arrest, but to teach, love and set free! He has experienced the "good news" firsthand. He goes from stoning Christians in Acts 7 to embracing them in Acts 9. He sees that God's plan in Christ for all of us is no longer just about what we can't do, but what we can do! He's now able to preach about resurrection, hope, forgiveness and a new life from firsthand experience.

> Rejoice in the Lord always. I will say it again: Rejoice!
> (Philippians 4:4)

The fact that this verse is a command baffles many people. How can you command a feeling, especially a feeling of joy? Considering most people's understanding of joy, that is a reasonable question. Do you remember last week's discussion on the difference between the world's definition of love and God's? The world's love is conditional and God's is unconditional; God expects us to love regardless of who the person is or what he or she does. The same is true of this fruit of the Spirit. Most people's joy is completely circumstantial. It is tied to their situation, mood and surroundings: one day their joy is up, the next day it is down. It shifts like the wind. Is it really possible to have so much control over your joy that you can have it every day (always)? Praise God the answer is yes! How is that possible?

> Finally, brothers, whatever is true, whatever is noble, whatever is right, whatever is pure, whatever is lovely, whatever is admirable—if anything is excellent or praiseworthy—think about such things. Whatever you have learned or received or heard from me, or seen in me—put it into practice. (Philippians 4:8–9)

The joy of the Spirit does not begin with a feeling, but an attitude. This reminds me of times when our very young children would whine and either Robyn or I would say to them, "Okay, it's time to get happy" or "Where is your happy face?" What we expected from them was that they needed to change their attitude and decide to let go of their whine and get happy. Believe it or not, it worked! They realized they really did have a choice.

Do you think that is God's expectation of us? Do you think that he is ready for us to get rid of the whine and get happy? It comes from deciding on whom ("in the _____" Philippians 4:4) and where ("think about such _____" Philippians 4:8b) your mindset will be.

I know that to some this sounds too simplistic; we cannot imagine that being joyful could be a decision away, but it can be! Let's face it: there are enough seemingly difficult things in any given day to make us miserable if we focus on them. The converse is also true; there are enough blessings in any given day to make us overflow with joy *if* we focus on them. I'm not preaching some pseudo-religious "power of positive thinking." Is there a power in thinking positively? Absolutely. But what Paul is speaking about here is so much deeper than that. A spiritual person is going to think about and concentrate on things that are true, noble, right, pure, lovely, admirable, excellent and praiseworthy! This is not a mind that is in the gutter. This is a mind that has decided to lift its eyes out of the ditch of defeat and hopelessness and see that there is so much more that God wants us to see. That is the path to unleashing the power of God to give you a joy that is inexplicable.

A word of caution: this joy will make no sense. It is like the paradox that Paul describes in 2 Corinthians 6:9–10: "beaten, and yet not killed; sorrowful, yet always rejoicing…having nothing, and yet possessing everything." How can you be "sorrowful, yet always rejoicing"? Was it that Paul's vision was so rose-colored that he could not see and feel compassion? Was he so calloused or macho that he experienced no pain or hurt? He does say "beaten." He freely admits, during those times he was "sorrowful." The fact is he experienced a pain and torture that few of us can imagine. Yet his "sorrow" during that time did not characterize him!

Through the power of the Holy Spirit, he refused to allow his circumstances to define him or his happiness: "beaten, and yet not killed…sorrowful, yet always rejoicing…." Wow, that calls me higher! There are days when I have to tell myself, "Bruce, change your mindset, focus on the blessings." Without the Spirit, my mindset can so easily focus on the challenges and the problems, not on the blessings and the promises. I hate to admit it, but there are times when I catch myself being negative. Through the years, I've learned that being negative never makes me feel better, only worse. I am thankful that through the Spirit, I have the power to get happy every day.

> I rejoice greatly in the Lord...for I have learned to be content whatever the circumstances. I know what it is to be in need, and I know what it is to have plenty. I have learned the secret of being content in any and every situation, whether well fed or hungry, whether living in plenty or in want. I can do everything through him who gives me strength. (Philippians 4:10–13)

Paul's "secret" to this kind of joy is this: he *learned* to be content *whatever*! Paul decided to see his life as an adventure. He was not someone who wallowed in a "woe is me" attitude; he loathed self-pity. He refused to be a victim. You never saw him whining. You never read where he uttered, "Why me?" I'm not saying he wasn't tempted or it was easy. He does say he *learned* the secret. Have you learned the secret of being content? Have you learned that real joy is not being content *if* this or that happens, but *whatever* happens? The fruit of the Spirit is joy.

Meditation and Discussion Questions

1. What calls you higher in the way that Paul looked at life?

2. Think about one or two disciples who most demonstrate this fruit of the Holy Spirit.
   - Who are they and how do they demonstrate the Spirit's fruit of joy?

3. Would you say that most people see you as a person who enjoys life?
   - If yes, why? If no, why not?

4. Are others drawn to your life, marriage and family because they see happiness?
   - If yes, why? If no, why not?

5. After looking at these passages in God's word, what would you say is the biggest block to your experiencing more of this particular fruit of the Spirit? Please be specific.

6. Think of situations in the last several weeks in which it was difficult for you to be joyful...
   - When you were victorious and joyful, what did you do or not do that enabled the Spirit of Christ to give you joy?

- When you were not victorious and joyful, what did you do or not do that kept the Holy Spirit from giving you joy?

7. Are there any possible challenges that you foresee coming this week that may potentially steal your joy?
   - What are they and what can you do to prepare for them?

WEEK FIVE

The Fruit of the Spirit is PEACE

> But the fruit of the Spirit is love, joy, *peace*, patience, kindness, goodness, faithfulness, gentleness and self-control.
> Galatians 5:22–23, emphasis added

This is the same peace that Jesus promises in John 14:27:

> "Peace I leave with you; my peace I give you. I do not give to you as the world gives. Do not let your hearts be troubled and do not be afraid."

Here we go again: another fruit of the Spirit that is in stark contrast to what the world knows. Most people's picture of peace is a day when the sky is azure blue, the sun is bright, the grass in the valley is emerald green, the temperature is 78 degrees, the lake is glassy calm and a bird sings sweetly in a tree that sways gently in the soft breeze. Got the picture? Sounds like most days in Southern California! Doesn't it make you want to just set up a hammock and take a snooze?

That is certainly one portrait of peace. But God's is different. This time the sky is dark and grey, the sun is blocked by the ominous buildup of clouds, the temperature has drastically dropped, the wind is howling at 74 miles per hour, bending the top of that same tree almost to the ground; but this time, that same bird is still sitting in that bent tree sweetly singing his song. Quite a contrast! But that's the difference!

> Do not be anxious about anything, but in everything, by prayer and petition, with thanksgiving, present your requests to God. And the _____ _____ _____, which transcends all understanding, will guard your _____ and your _____ in Christ Jesus. (Philippians 4:6–7)

Okay, I've got to be real here. Some days when I read this passage, my initial reaction is, "You have got to be kidding! 'Do not be anxious about _____?' What are you, from another planet?" This world is full of anxious folks! And some of us have to admit we feel like we are hard-wired to worry. We worry about what we have and don't have. We worry about what we do and don't do. We worry about what we know and don't know. It doesn't matter whether there is truly anything to worry about; no problem, we'll find something! Can you relate? If you can, then this fruit of the Spirit is custom-made for you.

God's Spirit specializes in giving us a peace "which passes all understanding." This peace has the power to " _____ your hearts and minds in Christ Jesus." When we get anxious, what follows is usually not very good. Anxiety quickly produces a lot of disasters. That is why the peace of the Spirit guards our hearts and minds. That peace is like a firewall that keeps the fire (anxiety) from jumping the line.

Have you ever had a wave of anxiety sweep over you that seemed to come out of nowhere? No explanation. It just hits. I have this picture in my mind of demons that belong to a "special force unit" of Satan. Their sole responsibility is to stress people out. You know what? They are very effective—even on disciples of Christ. Has Paul given us this impossible command? Do any of us stand a chance? The answer is simple: only if we obey the entire command.

If all we do is focus on not worrying, guess what? We'll fail! That is why the rest of the command is so vital: "but in everything, by_____ and _____, with _____ present your requests to God."

> He took Peter and the two sons of Zebedee along with him, and he began to be sorrowful and troubled. Then he said to them, "My soul is overwhelmed with sorrow to the point of death...."
> Going a little farther, he fell with his face to the ground and prayed, "My Father, if it is possible, may this cup be taken from me." (Matthew 26:37–39)

Sometimes the demons bombard us with anxious, negative or depressed feelings. These feelings seem so real and uncontrollable. ("...he began to be sorrowful and troubled.... 'My soul is overwhelmed with sorrow.') What do you think? Does it look like Jesus is being bombarded with demonic thoughts? The Bible says that he confesses in his prayer being "overwhelmed." Jesus is feeling it here. Yet again, we can see with Jesus' own life how he handled those demonic feelings. He prayed and surrendered. "Not my will, but yours be done." What an encouragement it should be to find out that God's Spirit actually empowers us to obey God!

God knows that we are going to have waves of anxious thoughts and feelings. Satan's demons will make sure of it! Prayer is the key. That is why we are commanded to "Cast all your _____ on him because he cares for you" (1 Peter 5:7). Do you cast all your anxieties on God? His shoulders are bigger and stronger than yours will ever be. Do you ask others to pray for you as well? That's the "petition" part of Philippians 4:6. I am confident that God has heard the faithful petitions that others have offered up to him on my behalf. Remember: this is a fruit of the Spirit that cannot be fully understood or explained...but it can be experienced.

Meditation and Discussion Questions

1. Think about the brothers or sisters who have demonstrated a peace that is not normal. Who were they and how did they demonstrate this peace?

2. What stands out to you about the way Jesus dealt with anxiety or situations that could have produced anxiety?

- In what ways will you make a commitment to imitate him in his response?

3. Think about the past month…
    - When you were victorious in being at peace, what did you do and not do that enabled the Holy Spirit to give you greater peace?

    - When you were not victorious in being at peace, what did you do and not do that prevented the Holy Spirit from giving you greater peace?

4. What are the areas that tempt you to be most anxious?

5. What will you do differently this week in order to express the fruit of peace?

– *Additional Notes* –

WEEK SIX

The Fruit of the Spirit is PATIENCE

> But the fruit of the Spirit is love, joy, peace, *patience*, kindness, goodness, faithfulness, gentleness and self-control.
> Galatians 5:22–23, emphasis added

Patience is also translated "longsuffering" or "forbearance" in other Bible translations. When Miles Coverdale translated the Bible into the English language in 1535, there was no English word equivalent to the actual Greek word; it was so unique that he believed he had to create the English word "longsuffering."

Since it is such a spiritual characteristic, you do not usually find this word outside the New Testament. However, it is used throughout the Old Testament as a characteristic of God, who is "slow to anger" (Numbers 14:18, Psalm 103:8, Jonah 4:2). This patience is the opposite of being "easily angered" (1 Corinthians 13:5). In Romans 2:4, Paul uses the same word to refer to God's *patience*. When you consider it, can you think of anyone who has been more patient with us than God? How many times did we deserve anything but patience from God? Yet, it was patience that we got.

> "O unbelieving and perverse generation," Jesus replied, "how long shall I stay with you? How long shall I put up with you? Bring the boy here to me." Jesus rebuked the demon, and it came out of the boy, and he was healed from that moment. (Matthew 17:17–18)

Moms and dads, we know what it's like to get frustrated with our children, right? Brothers and sisters, we also know what it's like to get annoyed with one another. Here was a situation where Jesus was on the edge of getting really irritated because of the disciples' lack of faith. He was open with his struggles and patiently dealt with the situation. There will be times in all of our lives when there are things people do or don't do that will irritate us. We have a choice at those times to either be patient or angry. I have made both choices. Jesus chose patience and used it as an opportunity to help the disciples to grow.

> As a prisoner for the Lord, then, I urge you to live a life worthy of the calling you have received. Be completely humble and gentle; be patient, bearing with one another in love. (Ephesians 4:1–2)

Patience is described here in Ephesians 4 as _____ _____ one another. Are we good at hanging in there with each other? We certainly are not going to learn that kind of patience from the world. The failed marriages and fractured families testify that many are better examples of quitting rather than persevering. However, when we look at God, we observe a very different example. God is so patient with us. Think about it: just how many times do you think you deserved to be zapped, but instead were forgiven? A hundred times? A thousand? How about countless? Are we as patient with one another as God is with us?

A person cannot survive in a family without a lot of patience. Many of us grew up in small families where we had a only a few siblings. Then when we came into God's family (the church), we were put into a family that is anything but small. Even our family groups are larger than most physical families. As you begin to build relationships with your brothers and sisters, you quickly see flaws and weaknesses that you had not noticed before. You may notice that some people may actually start to irritate you. What's the solution? Bailing? Moving on? That's not what we read in God's Book. He commands us to be patient.

Thinking about how patient God has been with me has motivated me many times to persevere with others when I had every "good" reason to quit. Don't you want to be motivated to keep your commitment to God's family from the heart? The more you think about the patience and perseverance that the Lord has never stopped giving to you, the stronger your inspiration is to hang in there and not give up.

The truth is, without patience no relationship of ours has any chance of survival. It is a foundational building block to any long term relationship. I'm glad it is a fruit of the Spirit.

Meditation and Discussion Questions

1. Think about the brothers or sisters who have demonstrated the greatest patience with you. Who were they and in what situations did they demonstrate patience?

2. What stands out to you about the way Jesus was patient?

- In what ways will you make a commitment to imitate him in his patience?

3. Think about the past month…
   - When you were victorious in being patient, what did you do and not do that enabled the Holy Spirit to give you greater patience?

   - When you were not victorious in being patient, what did you do and not do that prevented the Holy Spirit from giving you greater patience?

4. When are the times when you are most likely to "lose your patience"?

5. How do you want to respond differently in the future?

6. How does God's patience help you have patience with others?

7. Is there anyone that you need to apologize to for not being patient with them?

8. With whom are you committing to be more patient this week?

- What will you do differently in order to have the fruit of patience in this relationship?

– *Additional Notes* –

WEEK SEVEN

The Fruit of the Spirit is KINDNESS

> But the fruit of the Spirit is love, joy, peace, patience, *kindness*, goodness, faithfulness, gentleness and self-control.
> Galatians 5:22–23, emphasis added

This word in the Greek means "moral excellence, connoting strength of character." What do you think of when you think of kindness? Do you think of it as a characteristic of the weak and timid? If so, that certainly does not require God's Spirit! However, what if it were something almost the exact opposite? The best picture I have of kindness is one of an all-powerful giant choosing not to exert his power, but going out of his way to bend down and be gracious and gentle. "But when the kindness and love of God our Savior appeared, he saved us, not because of righteous things we had done, but because of his mercy" (Titus 3:4–5). Kindness is when someone has all the power for vengeance or retaliation but chooses not to use it.

> On one occasion an expert in the law stood up to test Jesus. "Teacher," he asked, "what must I do to inherit eternal life?"
>
> "What is written in the Law?" he replied. "How do you read it?"
>
> He answered: "Love the Lord your God with all your heart and with all your soul and with all your strength and with all your mind; and, Love your _____ as yourself."
>
> "You have answered correctly," Jesus replied. "Do this and you will live."
>
> But he wanted to justify himself, so he asked Jesus, "And who is my _____?"
>
> In reply Jesus said: "A man was going down from Jerusalem to Jericho, when he fell into the hands of robbers. They stripped him of his clothes, beat him and went away, leaving him half dead. A priest happened to be going down the same road, and when he saw the man, he passed by on the other side. So too,

a Levite, when he came to the place and saw him, passed by on the other side. But a Samaritan, as he traveled, came where the man was; and when he saw him, he took _____ on him. He went to him and bandaged his wounds, pouring on oil and wine. Then he put the man on his own donkey, took him to an inn and took care of him. The next day he took out two silver coins and gave them to the innkeeper. 'Look after him,' he said, 'and when I return, I will reimburse you for any extra expense you may have.'

"Which of these three do you think was a _____ to the man who fell into the hands of robbers?" The expert in the law replied, "The one who had mercy on him." Jesus told him, "Go and _____ _____." (Luke 10:25–37)

How would we rate ourselves on the kindness meter? Most of us might consider ourselves really kind people until we come to understand God's definition. I'll be honest: this story never ceases to challenge me; it is so simple and yet so powerfully convicting. Here were three different people who saw the same need. Two of them thought they had more to do than they could get done. I know that feeling. I'm sure all of us do. I see from this story that Jesus identified the opposite of kindness not as meanness, but as simply being calloused. Jesus chose to tell this story in response to the question to emphatically illustrate the second commandment: "Love your neighbor as yourself." His basic answer to "and who is my neighbor?" was, your neighbor is anyone you are around who has a need, whether you know the person or not.

According to this story, we who know God should be the kindest people in our neighborhoods and on our jobs. There is an organization that specializes in encouraging random acts of kindness. On their website (www.actsofkindness.org) there is a monthly calendar that lists suggested daily acts of kindness. We print that calendar for our family and put it on the wall for ideas of daily acts of kindness. Wouldn't it be great if we as individuals were known for our daily demonstrations of kindness? It could be as simple as introducing yourself to someone new, helping unload groceries, welcoming a new family to the neighborhood, preparing a meal for a family who is going through a medical recovery, or writing a thank-you note to someone who doesn't expect it.

> Husbands, in the same way be _____ as you live with your wives, and treat them with _____ as the weaker partner and as heirs with you of the gracious gift of life, so that nothing will hinder your _____. (1 Peter 3:7)

Most men are not naturally kind. We tend to be rough, rude, abrupt and insensitive. I thought I was a pretty nice guy until I got married; then I learned about kindness. I discovered that I can be mean and harsh and be totally oblivious to it. I realized, "Wow, I've got a lot to learn about kindness"; that was 32 years ago. I've grown in my kindness, but not without the Spirit. I'm hopelessly unkind without God and his Spirit alive and active in my life.

> In the same way, their wives are to be women worthy of respect, not _____ _____ but temperate and trustworthy in everything. (1 Timothy 3:11)

Women can also be unkind with their words. Gossip is one of the worst forms of unkindness. Careless words can tear down in one day what takes a lifetime to build. Perhaps more marriages have been shredded by words than anything else. ("Wives, in the same way be submissive to your husbands so that, if any of them do not believe the word, they may be won over _____ _____ by the _____ of their wives" 1 Peter 3:1.)

> Rather, as servants of God we commend ourselves in every way...in patience and _____; in the Holy Spirit and in sincere love. (2 Corinthians 6:4, 6)

I am encouraged that Paul believed he had become a kind person. There was certainly a time in his life when he was anything but kind. ("Even though I was once a blasphemer and a persecutor and a violent man…" 1 Timothy 1:13). By his own admission, Paul was a very violent man; however, because he was filled with the Holy Spirit, he became kind. He demonstrated that God's Spirit can give even the most un-kind-hearted person the ability to be so transformed that even Christians stand in awe. ("All those who heard him were astonished and asked, 'Isn't he the man who raised havoc in Jerusalem among those who call on this name?'" Acts 9:21.)

Meditation and Discussion Questions

1. How does God's kindness motivate you to show kindness to others?

2. How are you called higher by the way Jesus emphasized kindness?

3. Think about the brothers or sisters who have demonstrated the greatest kindness toward you or others.
    - Who were they and how did they demonstrate kindness?

4. Think about the past month…
   - When you were kind, what did you do and not do that enabled the Holy Spirit to give you greater kindness?

   - When you were not kind, what did you do and not do that prevented the Holy Spirit from helping you to be kinder?

5. What three things do you desire to accomplish this week by the power of the Holy Spirit?

– *Additional Notes* –

WEEK EIGHT

The Fruit of the Spirit is GOODNESS

> But the fruit of the Spirit is love, joy, peace, patience, kindness, *goodness*, faithfulness, gentleness and self-control.
> Galatians 5:22–23, emphasis added

Before studying the Bible and becoming a true Christian, most of us would have described ourselves as a good person. We would have compared ourselves to someone more wicked and evil than we were and would have concluded we looked pretty good; then we started reading the Bible. All those exaggerated views of our goodness faded quickly.

> For you were once darkness, but now you are light in the Lord. Live as children of light (for the fruit of the light consists in all _____, _____ and _____) and find out what pleases _____ _____. (Ephesians 5:8–10)

Goodness is certainly not something many people truly pursue today. Who wants to be considered a "goody two shoes"? In fact, being moral and righteous is so unpopular that many give the impression that they are not as good as they really are. Unmarried girls (and boys) are portrayed on teen TV shows as ashamed for still being virgins. The movie, *The 40 Year Old Virgin*, was a box office hit because it is about a 40-year-old man who needs help from his friends to overcome his "problem" of virginity. We certainly don't want to appear to be "too good for too long." How twisted is that?

As children of the light, we should be consumed with living a life that "pleases the Lord." God expects our lives "to consist in all goodness and righteousness." Even though we will never be perfect, goodness should be a life-long goal. It is a noble pursuit.

We must open our eyes and see that most people have abandoned their only reliable moral compass (God's word). Therefore, what was once understood to be unquestionably wrong is now considered acceptable. As children of God, we can never look to the world or compare our righteousness to the world's to define goodness. Characters in popular comedy shows joke about their friends' number of casual one-night stands. Famous singers who claim morals and religious beliefs dance lewdly in music videos. Trusted accounting firms are exposed for falsifying records.

In this Ephesians 5 passage, Paul declares that goodness is not just a fruit of the Spirit, but also "a fruit of the _____." From experience, we all know that to be true. The more real and open we are about our lives (live in the light), the greater the opportunity we have to truly develop goodness. I am a better man, husband, father, brother and leader when I am open with my life. The reason that there is such emphasis on confession and openness to one another in the Scriptures is that when you have the Holy Spirit, evil has no chance of either getting a foothold or thriving. That would only happen in the darkness.

All successful programs that help people overcome their addictions do so by utilizing the tools of openness and accountability. We are very blessed here in LA to have numerous ministries that have successfully helped people who were enslaved to drugs, alcohol or sexual impurity. There is a reason why certain sinful activities are classified as "deeds of darkness" (Romans 13:12, Ephesians 5:11). These ministries have story after story of brothers and sisters who had given up on ever being "good" again, but goodness came into their lives once they made the decision to be children of the light.

> I myself am convinced, my brothers, that you yourselves are _____ of _____. (Romans 15:14)

Can you imagine yourself to ever be "full of goodness"? Don't count it out. We can become so much like Jesus that we can overflow with goodness. Brothers, believe that the Spirit's power is there to help you to become a better man than you ever thought possible. Sisters, believe that the Holy Spirit is there to help you become a more spiritual woman than you ever dreamed. The fruit of the Spirit is…goodness.

The Fruit of the Spirit is GOODNESS

Meditation and Discussion Questions

1. What has been your attitude toward goodness?

2. What do you believe God would have you do in order to empower the Holy Spirit to make you full of goodness?

3. What things in the world have you allowed to affect your desire for goodness?

4. What can you do to keep the world's influence from affecting your standard of goodness?

5. How can we as fellow Christians help one another in our pursuit of goodness?

– *Additional Notes* –

WEEK NINE

The Fruit of the Spirit is FAITHFULNESS

> But the fruit of the Spirit is love, joy, peace, patience, kindness, goodness, *faithfulness*, gentleness and self-control.
> Galatians 5:22–23, emphasis added

Although this word primarily is used in the context of moral conviction, it can also be used to convey perseverance in our commitment to Christ and his church. "We do not want you to become lazy, but to imitate those who through faith and patience inherit what has been promised" (Hebrews 6:12). Faithfulness requires courage and moral fortitude.

> But we are not of those who shrink back and are destroyed, but of those who believe and are saved. (Hebrews 10:39)

Faithfulness is fundamental to making it to heaven. If faithfulness is so essential to spending eternity with the Lord, then it stands to reason that we need the grace of God to be saved and the grace and Spirit of God to persevere and stay saved. This faithfulness is the condition in which we remain forgiven and showered with grace:

> But now he has reconciled you by Christ's physical body through death to present you holy in his sight, without blemish and free from accusation—if you continue in your _____, established and firm, not _____ from the hope held out in the gospel. (Colossians 1:22–23)

This same word for faithfulness in the Greek *(pistis)* is used numerous times to convey loyalty to our foundational beliefs:

> I...delight to see how orderly you are and how firm your _____ in Christ is.

> So then, just as you received Christ Jesus as Lord, continue to live in him, _____ and built up in him, strengthened in the _____ as you were taught. (Colossians 2:5–7)

> For this reason...I sent to find out about your _____.
> (1 Thessalonians 3:5)

God expects his children to have convictions that remain deeply rooted and unshakeable. It is a fact that some of us have deeper convictions than others. The good news is that through consistent study of the Word, we can all develop a deeper commitment to Biblical doctrine that cannot be "blown here and there by every wind of teaching and by the cunning and craftiness of men in their deceitful scheming" (Ephesians 4:14).

> ...but to show that they can be fully _____ *[pistis]* so that in every way they will make the teaching about God our Savior attractive. (Titus 2:10)

There is also an aspect of this fruit that connotes reliability. Disciples with this fruit can be counted on by those in authority over them. Keeping our commitments is an essential part of being a true disciple of Christ. Are you the kind of employee that your employer can count on day in and day out? Through the years, I have witnessed the reputation of many disciples being so reliable on their jobs that their employers wanted to know if there were more people that they could hire from the church! That is putting faithfulness into action.

Meditation and Discussion Questions

1. How did studying these passages on faithfulness affect your convictions about the importance of this fruit of the Spirit?

2. Why is it so crucial to be faithful to both Christ and his church?

3. Are you steadfast in the Biblical doctrines you were taught when you became a Christian?
   - Which doctrines have you been tempted to compromise?

   - Are there any doctrines that you need to develop a deeper understanding and conviction about? What are they and what will you do to make that happen?

4. What two changes in the area of reliability do you need to make either at home or at work?

– Additional Notes –

WEEK TEN

The Fruit of the Spirit is GENTLENESS

> But the fruit of the Spirit is love, joy, peace, patience, kindness, goodness, faithfulness, *gentleness* and self-control.
> Galatians 5:22–23, emphasis added

This is one of the few times when the New International translation does not adequately translate this Greek word *prautes* (pronounced prah-oo'-tace) from the root word *praus,* which is usually translated as "humble" or "meek" (Matthew 5:5). It is used only four times in the entire New Testament. The other three passages where it is used are the following:

> Therefore, get rid of all moral filth and the evil that is so prevalent and _____ accept the word planted in you, which can save you. (James 1:21)

> Who is wise and understanding among you? Let him show it by his good life, by deeds done in the _____ that comes from wisdom. (James 3:13)

> But in your hearts set apart Christ as Lord. Always be prepared to give an answer to everyone who asks you to give the reason for the hope that you have. But do this with _____ and respect. (1 Peter 3:15)

As you can see in these other three passages, the context conveys that humility is either translated or implied. We know how fundamentally necessary humility is to come to know God (Matthew 18:2–4). Remember what a great victory it was to truly have godly sorrow for the first time? That type of humility is key to becoming more and more like Jesus.

We are commanded in James 1:21 to "humbly accept the word planted in [us]." When the word is preached or taught, it is planted in you.

Have you ever found yourself struggling to be humble when hearing the truth? As a younger man, when someone pointed out something that I needed to change, I have to admit that most of the time I was tempted to be defensive and too many times *became* defensive. I needed the Holy Spirit just to take the correction with a spiritual attitude!

Most of us are not naturally inclined to respond with humility when challenged. I have learned through the years that defensiveness blocks others' communication and openness with me as well as preventing my growth. Before we have any hope of changing whatever we are being challenged to change, we first need to see we have some things to change; that requires humility. How encouraging it is to realize that humility is a fruit of the Spirit!

Meditation and Discussion Questions

1. Think about the past month…
   - When you were victorious in being humble, what did you do and not do that enabled the Holy Spirit to give you greater humility?

   - When you were not victorious in being humble, what did you do and not do that prevented the Holy Spirit from giving you greater humility?

2. Is there anyone you need to apologize to for not being humble with them?

3. To whom are you committing to be more humble this week? (Name several.)

- What will you do differently in order to have this fruit?

4. Do you pray for humility? When is the last time you experienced God answering your prayer for more humility?

– Additional Notes –

WEEK ELEVEN

The Fruit of the Spirit is SELF-CONTROL

> But the fruit of the Spirit is love, joy, peace, patience, kindness, goodness, faithfulness, gentleness and *self-control*.
> Galatians 5:22–23, emphasis added

We have come to the ninth and final fruit mentioned here in Galatians 5. It is not a surprise that Paul completes his list with "self-control." Without control of self, there is no hope to develop spirituality.

> Then Jesus was led by the Spirit into the desert to be tempted by the devil. After fasting forty days and forty nights, he was hungry. The tempter came to him and said, "If you are the Son of God, tell these stones to become bread." Jesus answered, "_____ _____ _____: 'Man does not live on bread alone, but on every word that comes from the mouth of God.'" (Matthew 4:1–4)

> Very early in the morning, while it was still _____ Jesus _____ _____, left the house and went off to a solitary place, where he prayed. (Mark 1:35)

> For we do not have a high priest who is unable to sympathize with our weaknesses, but we have one who has been tempted in _____ _____, just as we are—yet was without sin. (Hebrews 4:15)

Throughout the Gospels, we see Jesus exercise a consistent mastery of self. Whether it was controlling his hunger and fasting for 40 days, resisting every conceivable temptation hurled at him, or getting up before sunrise to commune with his heavenly Father, Jesus' life demonstrated the power of the Holy Spirit to give a man self-control. The Hebrews passage above makes it clear that Jesus was not some spiritual robot who was insulated from real flesh-and-blood temptations. We read how Jesus throughout each day wrestled the demons to the ground through prayer and the Holy Spirit.

Going a little farther, he fell with his face to the _____ and _____, "My Father, if it is possible, may this cup be taken from me. Yet not as I will, but as _____ _____."

Then he returned to his disciples and found them sleeping. "Could you men not keep watch with me for one hour?" he asked Peter. "_____ and _____ so that you will not fall into temptation. The spirit is willing, but the body is weak."

He went away a _____ time and prayed, "My Father, if it is not possible for this cup to be taken away unless I drink it, may your will be done."

When he came back, he again found them sleeping, because their eyes were heavy. So he left them and went away once more and prayed the _____ time, saying the same thing.

Then he returned to the disciples and said to them, "Are you still sleeping and resting? Look, the hour is near, and the Son of Man is betrayed into the hands of sinners. Rise, let us go! Here comes my betrayer!" (Matthew 26:39–46)

Throughout my 36 years as a Christian, I've heard disciples make many excuses for why they were not more spiritual. One excuse given by many was, "I'm not as naturally spiritual as this brother or that sister." During those times, I guess they were thinking that I would just think to myself, "Oh, really? That's too bad God didn't give you the 'spirituality' gene." Do you know anyone with this "spirituality" gene? In all seriousness, this kind of excuse demonstrates a tremendous ignorance of what it takes to truly become spiritual.

Another excuse I've heard is, "Wow, spirituality comes so much easier for you than it does for me." Oh, really? That's like saying to a person that works out every day at the gym, "Muscle tone comes so much easier to you than it does to me."

The truth is, ease and genetics have nothing to do with spirituality. Being spiritual comes from making every effort to exercise self-control by the power of the Holy Spirit. At the very end of Jesus' life, he

The Fruit of the Spirit is SELF-CONTROL

was faced with his greatest challenge. He knew it was coming. He knew it was going to be rugged. He would be beaten, tortured and crucified with spikes in his hands and feet. He would be despised, rejected, shunned and denied even by his most ardent disciples.

How do you face something like that? Does it sound like just another day? Notice, his control of self included taking his three closest disciples in the middle of the night to a solitary place to stay up with him; he needed their intercessory prayers. He threw himself on the ground before God, the Father. He prayed his own loud and blood-strained prayers! "During the days of Jesus' life on earth, he offered up prayers and petitions with _____ _____ and _____" (Hebrews 5:7).

> And being in anguish, he prayed more _____, and his sweat was like drops of _____ falling to the ground. (Luke 22:44)

What does it look like to you? Does it sound like spirituality came naturally? That is not what I read. These passages tell me that Jesus' spirituality took work, prayer and openness. Remember: "He _____ obedience from what he suffered" (Hebrews 5:8). You do not learn something that comes naturally. It would be a grave mistake to interpret Jesus' spirituality as something that came automatically.

> For this very reason, make every effort to add to your faith goodness; and to goodness, knowledge; and to knowledge, self-control; and to _____-_____, perseverance; and to perseverance, godliness. (2 Peter 1:5–6)

The apostle Peter uses the same exact word for self-control here that Paul used in Galatians 5. God expects us to grow in our self-control. There is an obvious control of self that is demonstrated in initially becoming a Christian. You can probably recall many changes that you made as a new Christian that were made possible by Biblically produced convictions, the receiving the Holy Spirit, and the new discovery of self-control. As we mature, the need for deep and strong self-control increases. We will become more and more aware of every crack and weak spot in our lives. These cannot be overcome without the Holy Spirit's power of self-control.

I've needed self-control today; in fact, I've had lots of "opportunities" to practice it. I had a sore throat and was in a grumpy mood and was tempted to snap at my wife. I could not find several items for a trip I was already late leaving for. Someone broke a promise he had made to me, and someone procrastinated in a way that affected me. Another day it could be other things: someone was defensive toward me, and someone cut me off in traffic. I was offered an extra helping of my favorite food, and I was having trouble going to bed on time or getting up on time. God had said no to a specific prayer and I couldn't figure out why. Take your pick. You see, every day brings many opportunities for self-control. I am so thankful that I have divine power to grow in control of self.

> Now the Lord is the Spirit, and where the Spirit of the Lord is, there is freedom. And we, who with unveiled faces all reflect the Lord's glory, are being _____ into his likeness with _____ - _____ glory, which comes from the Lord, who is the _____. (2 Corinthians 3:17–18)

As we noted at the very beginning of this series, we have the amazing Spirit of God living inside of us. His Spirit is longing to transform us into his likeness and is powerful enough to do just that. We saw that what we really needed to be praying for was not more power, but for more surrender, more desire to see this resurrection power work in our lives, more passion to be spiritual and to deny self to let God's Spirit make this transformation a reality for us.

Meditation and Discussion Questions

1. What stands out to you about the way Jesus demonstrated self-control?

The Fruit of the Spirit is SELF-CONTROL

- In what ways will you make a commitment to imitate him in his self control?

2. How does the world tempt us to believe that self-control is impossible?

3. Think about the brothers or sisters who have been an example of self-control. Who are they and how did they demonstrate it?

4. Name two main areas in which you need more self-control.

- How can you depend more on God's power to be controlled in these areas?

- What specific ways will you follow Jesus' example to grow in self-control?

- What will you do differently in order to have this fruit?

5. Is there anyone that you need to apologize to for your lack of self-control with them?

EPILOGUE

WALKING IN THE SPIRIT

> So I say, live by the Spirit, and you will not gratify the desires of the sinful nature.... Since we live by the Spirit, let us keep in step with the Spirit.
>
> Galatians 5:16, 25

What could be greater than to deeply realize that you have been forgiven of every sin, given a new life, and now have the very presence and power of God Almighty inside of you every day with every step you take? The only thing greater would be to escape the entrapment of this fleshly body and be given a glorious new body (1 Corinthians 15:35ff).

But while we are in this body, we have temptations and challenges that confront us every day. We have seen through this series that we have been given more than enough power to be victorious and godly. God has called us to "live by the Spirit."

> Those who live according to the sinful nature have their minds set on what that nature desires; but those who live in accordance with the Spirit have their minds set on what the Spirit desires. (Romans 8:5–6)

According to this passage, God says the key to living by the Spirit is having our "minds set on what the Spirit desires." As Christians, pleasing the Lord must be our number one priority daily. I have been asked many times, "How have you stayed faithful and continued to grow all these years as a disciple?" Every morning, I make every effort to mentally renew that pledge I made to Christ 36 years ago to deny myself and take up his cross daily. I try to follow Jesus' example in the Garden, where he focused more on God's will than his own.

Our walk on this earth will not be perfect. In fact, there will be days when it seems like the more areas you change, the more your weaknesses increase. That probably is not true; it is more likely that you are just becoming more sensitized to what it really means to be like Christ.

Prayerfully this study has already begun to help you to understand more completely what it truly means to please the Lord. While certainly not the only key, a deeper understanding of the power and fruit of his Spirit helps me set my mind on what the Spirit desires.

God deeply desires to fill with his refreshing Holy Spirit every soul who repents and is baptized for the forgiveness of sins (Acts 2:38). We have to remember that God desires such a personal and uninterrupted relationship with each one of us, that he not only gave his son to be crucified to wash us clean from our filthy sins, but he has put his amazing presence in our bodies, and now we have become his temples.

God wants to do great things through you. He wants to use you to draw and lead many others to know him. He wants to bless and work through your life to, in turn, bless others. Allow yourself to be led by the Spirit by setting your mind on pleasing God, and he will do "even greater things" (John 14:12). Remember: you have the power and fruit of the Holy Spirit!

Meditation and Discussion Questions

1. What truth from this series has made the most impact on your life? Why?

2. What do you believe will be necessary to maintain a life that is led by the Spirit and that keeps growing?

Printed in the United States
200518BV00002B/1-105/A